An Eye
Of The
Storm

An Eye Of The Storm

Katrina B. Ellis

XULON PRESS

Xulon Press
2301 Lucien Way #415
Maitland, FL 32751
407.339.4217
www.xulonpress.com

© 2020 by Katrina B. Ellis

All rights reserved solely by the author. The author guarantees all contents are original and do not infringe upon the legal rights of any other person or work. No part of this book may be reproduced in any form without the permission of the author. The views expressed in this book are not necessarily those of the publisher.

Paperback ISBN-13: 978-1-6322-1306-8
Ebook ISBN-13: 978-1-6322-1307-5

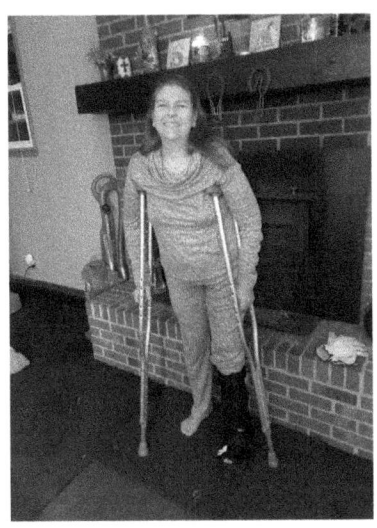

The Lord's Prayer

*Our Father who art in heaven hallowed be thy name.
Thy kingdom come, thy will be done, on earth as it is
in heaven.
Give us this day our daily bread and forgive our trespasses, as we forgive those who trespass against us.
Lead us not into temptation but deliver us from evil.
For thine is the kingdom, the power, and the glory,
for ever and ever.*

Amen

Let me start with when I was born; it was May 11, 1978. I was born in a small town called Morganton in North Carolina, as the hospital is Grace Hospital! The nurse who delivered me was Gena Singleton and she had to resuscitate me. Can you Believe THAT? I was dead, but by the grace of something, I came back! My birth name was Tina Lane and I was handed to my mother, Helen Epley, afterwards. My mother put a man's name on my birth certificate, and his name was Billy Black. I'm not sure if he is my father or not. Back then, while growing up, I didn't know him.

I grew up in an even smaller town called Glen Alpine, North Carolina! My mother's name was Helen Epley, as you know, while her mother's and father's names were Mary and Boonie South. Boonie would beat on us and Mary switched us. Of course, I always ran far, far away, just like Jenny said to do from the movie Forrest Gump! Sometimes I'd be gone for days.

My mother had two sisters named Linda and Betty Joe . Linda has two daughters and a mentally-challenged son. Their names are Christy, Caren, and Richard. As I know of, Linda now lives in Glen Alpine, North Carolina . I asked her about two years ago....because I'm brave... "Are you still burning down your HOMES?" She didn't particularly like that comment and blocked me on her Facebook page! I'm no longer speaking to my aunt. She is as evil as the rest of the family.

Christy is in a total mess! She moved away from them and is somewhere in Glen Alpine. Caren, you ask? I found out not too long ago that she is actually Christy's child. What do you think about them apples?! As far as I know, they still live with Linda and Caren has children of her own now. What about Richard, you ask? Just like the rest, he lives at Linda's. He is my age, forty-one, soon to be forty-two! By the grace of something, he is still living! Linda likes the money, as you can see.

Betty Joe has two sons, Justin and Tylor. The one I grew up with is named Justin and, last I knew, he now lives in Virginia. He finally got away.

Tylor is in and out of jail, running from the police. He is also... you guessed it... at Linda's.

My mother also had three brothers named Bill, Paul, and Jackie . They were all drunk and in and out of jail.

Bill owned a honky tonk and a junkyard that was on the property. He has a daughter named Amana Sue. He would come over the pathways that led from trailer to trailer, just to cause a fight with my mother and the man I called "Daddy." One day, Bill? He had a gun! My dog and me were on the front porch and he put the gun between its eyes. Can you believe that? He said my dog barked too much. Another day, he took Daddy by the back of his head and drug him out and off the porch. The only reason Bill did this was because he was drunk and couldn't find my mother. See, Daddy couldn't protect himself because he had polio; of course I didn't know what that was then. Bill drug him on the gravel road of Chambers Chapel Circle on his bare back. The police and ambulance soon came. I always ran away and hid when things like this happened. Once again, by the grace of something, I survived.

Paul was mean too He eventually moved to a town called Chesterfield, on the other side of Morganton. I lived with him for a while and he would beat up anyone he could, including his wife and daughter! I always tried to run. He was just like the rest of them, drunk. I remember walking a mile down to the bus stop when I went to school! I liked it though. You see, there was a store across the street and I would go in and steal my favorite candy bar, Zero. I would run back to the trailer park and hide in the woods to eat it. That way, it never was taken away from me. Paul's daughter was named Punky; not sure why she was named that. That's what I knew her as and I had to take care of her some.

Then, there's Jackie. I remember he married a woman named Robin but other than that, I don't remember him much. You see, he was always in jail.

Everyone in the family was drunk off Old Milwaukee or high from whatever they could get their hands on. They went to jail all the time. Us kids were given alcohol; plus, we stole their weed. When they weren't in jail, they loved to pass us kids out to each other and they messed with us sexually. Incest at its finest.

Back to Amanda Sue, Bill's daughter. She was my best friend and we were inseparable! We went in the junk cars and busses to play. One day, we decided we would get in a car. I pulled the gear shift. Oh no, what a mistake! It started rolling down the hill. I jumped out of the window, but Amanda still was inside of the car. I ran away for the entire day, because I was afraid Bill was going to beat the HELL out of me. He never found me though, so yay for me. Another day we went through a bus and found a knife. Amanda, or Mandy as I called her, jabbed me in my left cheek. She now lives in Marion, North Carolina. She never was around the sex stuff so she didn't know what was happening to us.

My mother had three children before I was born: their names are Kay, Misty/Felicia, and Jimmy ! They were taken away from her by DSS before I was born. I knew them a little because of school. They went to the high school beside my school. They made sure I got to eat as I never had anything to eat otherwise. My family used my check for beer and cigarettes.

She had another child who was adopted within her family. His name was Ernie Lane and he molested me at the age of eight or nine; I don't remember my exact age at the time. He took me to the woods and tried to have sex with me. It hurt so I squirmed and tried yelling. He then had me put my mouth on his thing!!! He held my head down until he shot something in. Another time, he filled a water gun with his pee and shot it in my mouth. Yuck. I spit it out.

My mother married a man named Gary Epley, I guess, before I was born. I called him Daddy, as he was the only father I knew. He took as good enough care of me that he could. He was born with polio, which I didn't know what it was then. He was disabled from it, as his left arm was positioned as though in a sling and he had a limp. He also has cognitive issues. He would walk me to school when I went. I was at Glen Alpine Elementary and had to ride bus 64! I was constantly dirty and had huge bugs crawling in my head. When I went to school, every one made fun of me. I was always hungry and had to steal anything for me to eat. No one would feed me. I had to help fix Daddy up also, as he was constantly beaten up by my mother. I was in a constant survival mode. We moved around, or I was shifted around the family, in order for DSS not to take me away. We never had power and my mother would be constantly drunk and go into rages. One time, I remember her throwing a MaxWell House coffee jar at his face and cut his eyebrow open. Blood was oozing out. I had to, once again, fix him. The ambulance and police came that time. I don't remember what happened after that. You see? I am still putting puzzle pieces together about my life.

The last place I really remember living was in a place called Howard Davis's Salvage Trailer Park. Howard rented out two trailers. My mother tried to pawn me off into prostitution, but I always ran away from her. I was friends with a boy next door; we went to a field for me to show him how a woman and a man perform in bed. I thought this is what we were supposed to do, but we got interrupted by his mom calling him to eat. We would climb trees too. I fell out once; don't remember that too much because I think I got knocked out. I remembered that I lost my breath, but I got up to do it again.

I was told to break into the neighbor's trailer and steal valuables to bring back to my mother. They called the police department and they investigated, to which the police traced it back to me. They found my dirty footprints on their bed. I was so afraid I was going to get locked up, but the police said since I was a minor, they were not going to press charges. WOW. I was scared to death. No one went to jail! I would steal chickens and the eggs from Howard, the landlord. He called the police so many times, and I was scared of getting locked up more times than I can remember.

Then, THANKS to my fourth-grade teacher of Glen Alpine Elementary, Mr. David McGee, I was saved. He called DSS and reported my nastiness: my dirty body, filthy clothes, and the HUGE BUGS in my head.

DSS had already had me joined with The Big Brothers/Big Sisters program. I met the most wonderful person in the entire world through it. You will never believe me if I told you. Gena Singleton: The first time I met her, I told her, "I love you," and waved bye. I was with Linda then and wanted Gena so badly to rescue me. I didn't want her to disappear like Bob and Kelly did! Bob and Kelly just stopped picking me up. NaNa is what I called her and then I had to sit at the dining room table after we got to her house and do my homework. We worked tirelessly on multiplying and dividing.

Anyway, back to Mr. McGee. Like I said, he called DSS. DSS came out to investigate and I told my mother to tell them what Ernie had done to me. Why she did I'll never understand. My social worker, Lisa , took me in her car so I could give her the gruesome details. I had to explain that my own brother tried having sex with me. Thank God he was too big. So he had me get on top of him and suck on it. Yuck. Lisa asked me if I were to be adopted, then who would I want it to be. Thank you Mr. McGee. My eyes lit up like a Christmas tree. I, IMMEDIATELY, said, "Gena Singleton!!!" Lisa talked to Gena about it. Without hesitation, Gena Singleton said yes. Finally, I was saved in 1994. Here I come, baby.

I called her NaNa, as you know! She put me in the bath and scrubbed my head for hours! Wouldn't you know it? Those bugs went away, FINALLY!!! I stopped itching She took my earrings out. OUCH. I finally had my new family. I took swimming lessons at The Morganton Recreation Department. I learned how to swim Then, fall came. NaNa had a house on Forest Hill Street; it was huge. She also enrolled me in her neighborhood school.

Forest Hill Elementary was where I was a big fifth-grader. I was in a fourth/fifth grade combination class, which was taught by my favorite teacher, Mrs. Williams. She had us write a letter to ourselves on how our summer went. Mine was great, as I was being adopted. I loved math and science and made SOO many friends.

Gena introduced me to ALL her friends. I didn't know how to act. They threw me the biggest party. NaNa said it was for my adoption; I was so happy. Then NaNa introduces me to her family and I met my new grandma and grandpa. Then? The UNBELIEVABLE THING HAPPENED. Mommy came out of my mouth when I talked to her. She hugged me and told me, "I LOVE YOU!" I said that a long time ago!!! I was finally safe.

Mommy had to take me back to DSS though. They were trying to do some sort of reunification with my birth family! I didn't want to go. I went to my "new" family reunion and they told me something BIG. They said I was one of them now.

DSS was trying to do this so-called "Family Reunification!" That's when DSS tries to make the biological family unit work. Sometimes it is just best to let it be! I hated every moment of it. I cried, kicking and screaming, because I just didn't want to go. "Those" people, as I called them, would bring me big, black garbage bags full of stuff. I hated everything about it! Every time after a visit, I would "act up" just to see how much Mommy would take. Mommy loved me no matter what. She taught me how to speak and how to act. She even taught me how to be a lady. Mommy put me in therapy to help me.

I met a really nice man named Lory. He was neat and I liked him. He helped me get through this adoption stuff. I asked him to find out about my father, because I never knew him, just that he was on my birth certificate: Billy Black! I surely didn't want him to take me. I just wanted to know who he was. Lory contacted and found him in Liberty, North Carolina. He made an appointment to meet me. I was scared. I went to the therapy appointment and....he never showed up. UGG!!! I wanted to know what I looked like from him. Where do my small hands come from? What about my small feet? I didn't know. I was wanting to ask him why he didn't want me; why he left me to suffer with my family??? I had SOOO many questions to ask him. I was really angry with him. So, the BIG DAY finally came: I was going to be adopted. Then Thanksgiving break came and all of Mom's family came. They loved me. You know something else? I loved them.

Lory helped me go in front of the judge and tell him what happened to me. I was ready. But wait, what happens next? That family lawyer convinced her to let me go. I WAS FREEEE. UNBELIEVABLE!!! I literally jumped up and down with joy. It was over and it took me a while to get used to being in a safe and secure place, let alone have a family to love me. I had a grandma and grandpa; aunts and uncles who weren't mean. WOW. We celebrated holidays for the very first time. My first Christmas with my new family was hard! Christmas Eve was here and a knock came at the door. I looked at Mommy and asked who it was. She told me to open it and you will never believe who it was. It was... Santa!!!

He leaned down to me and said, "I'm so sorry that I've missed your house the past few years. I promise you I will never ever forget you again!" I couldn't believe it! Santa made me the biggest promise. Soon Christmas morning came. Mommy had to get me up. She said, "Go look to see what Santa brought you." I did, dragging my feet. I looked all around. Try guessing what I got. I got...a bike, TEN SPEED!!! I got clothes, BRAND NEW!!! I got shoes, LA Gears!!! I Got Barbies, from a STORE!!! I couldn't believe HOW MUCH STUFF I got. SANTA DIDN'T LET ME DOWN!!! Then back to school I went.

I worked my butt off at school. I remember having a field day. I beat a girl in basketball; her name was Katie . I STILL have the blue ribbon. I got my first report card; this was in 1995. I ran all the way home, yelling the whole time, "Mommy, Mommy." She opened the door and asked, "What is wrong???" I said, "LOOK!!!" She did and saw all As and one B. I DID IT, yay for me. I got the B in reading, which I couldn't comprehend.

So, the summer came, and I was going to the library to learn how to read better. I was going to the rec. I was even babysitting. Can you believe that?! I wanted to work, so Mom helped me get a job. Can you guess where??? The Morganton Recreation Dept. They told me to get in the pool and see what I could do. I was a swimming instructor at age fourteen. MOMMY? She even had a vacation planned: We went to Maryland. I never had gone out of the state. I even got to go...can you guess... to Disney World. WOW!!! Fall of 1995 came and I was a big ninth-grader. I had just finished teaching swimming lessons at the pool and was fifteen!

I went to Freedom High School with 2 000+ students. I was so excited and joined a club called...what else...The Spirit Club. I was also in German class and in 1996, I joined the marching band . I was on the flag core and we were the best, with 200+ marching. We went under Mr. Justice. That Christmas was unreal. I got a car from my new Auntie Helen. I couldn't believe my eyes. Some friends and I drove it across country. It was from California, a Blue Ford Probe. I got my license on my birthday and drove to school in my new car.

I met a boy and asked him if he wanted to go roller skating with me. He said yes; his name was Alexander. German. We were so in love. I gave him a middle name because Germans don't have one. We dated through three years of high school and he graduated while I was still a junior and had to go back to Germany. I rode with his host family to take him to the airport in Charlotte. We took a moment in the tunnel to the door, said we loved each other, kissed, and cried The doors locked behind him. I kept his necklace! He let me wear it while he and I dated! We called each other every day. I was finally HAPPY!!! That next Christmas was great, as Mommy let me go to Germany to visit Alex, all by MYSELF. I was sixteen, drinking age in Germany. In band, we always snuck around and drank. But, this time I was legal.

I flew into the Stuttgart Airport, which is in the Black Forest area of Germany. They picked me up and drove me to Ruteshiem, where they lived. I stayed at his house, met his mom and dad. It was great. I went upstairs to get settled and take a nap. They are six hours behind us in time. I woke up and came down to see he had another girl standing in front of him. And you won't BELIEVE what her name was?! An Katrine, the same name as me. Alex told me about her some, but I didn't know it was serious.

I was PISSED, ran upstairs, and called my mommy to say I was coming back. I wanted to come home. However, we didn't have the money though, so I did what anyone else would do and made the best out of the two weeks. Alex, An Katrine, and myself went to see a movie, Terminator 3, in German even. Alex was in the middle, and that was the first and last time I saw her. Thank God.

We got back to his house and guess who was there?! My German teacher, Joe Koener. I couldn't believe it. Koener was Alex's uncle, if you remember me telling you that earlier. Also, his host brother was there, Clark Erwin. He was a rich jerk. Anyway, Alex's parents took us to visit his grandparents. They were in Achern. I knew all about Achern, so I was excited. You see? The other German exchange students are from there. I had many friends there and my ex-boyfriend! We got there and visited his grandparents. Then Alex, his mom, and me went across the border into Strasbourg, France: got some wonderful perfume, went to lunch, and they had dogs sitting at the tables eating. They ordered an appetizer, escargot. Alex DIDN'T tell me what I was going to eat. He told me to open my mouth and take a bite. It was great. He later told me that I ate snails. I loved them anyway.

After lunch, we decided to shop some. Then an ice storm hit and we had to get back to Achern, Germany. So we got to the bottom of the mountain to Alex's grandparents and had to park the car. Slipping and sliding, we made it across the road to a neighbor's house. They told us to put socks over our shoes. They gave us the socks. Then? What do you think we did, the three of us?? We hiked up the mountain. Finally, we made it to our destination. It was nighttime and we were tired. Alex called his cousin, who I knew, and she was having a birthday party. Alex and I got dressed and started walking down the mountain. I decided to get down on my butt, so I slid down to the bottom. Alex followed my lead and we made it to our ride and the party.

All of the foreign exchange students I knew were there, including my ex-boyfriend!!! They gave me a real German beer. It was warm, so I asked them to put some in the refrigerator for me. Alex did and I proceeded to drink like a fish. Then? You won't believe me. They wanted to go to the club I've always heard about. It was called "The Why Not!" I remember getting my coat and gloves on, sliding on the porch, and saying, "Oooh, I'm ice skating!" I must have blacked out then because I came to at the club. I asked to use the toilet. Don't remember how I got there, but I was hugging the toilet. Then I blacked out again and came to on a cot. I asked Alex why everybody left and started crying. I thought I ruined the party but Alex comforted me and lights out!. I passed out till morning.

An Eye Of The Storm

The next morning was hell, because I had the worst headache. Alex's parents gave me a couple of pills to help. I was so embarrassed and was sick. Alex said that I was speaking fluent German. Wow, I couldn't believe that. Then Alex's dad drove us back to Ruteshiem. Alex and I spent the rest of the time looking at castles and where he grew up. Then? Can you guess? Alex gave me a ring, a small diamond. It was gorgeous. He said that it was just a ring, but I told him that he gave me a promise ring. I made sure I knew it was just a ring, but of course I didn't.

I flew back with his host brother, Clark. Uggg!!! He was a jerk. I almost got stuck at customs too. They thought I was going to blow up the plane or something! My hair brush was Butane. They finally let me through as long as I kept it up. Clark and I were closely seated, watched WaterWorld, and drank. When we got back, I made myself disappear from him. All in all, I have to say that was the best trip ever. I talked to Alex every day, and then Valentine's came.

I told Alex he had to choose between me and An Katrine. He wouldn't, so I did. I told him goodbye and threw off my ring; lost it actually. My heart was shattered in 1997. I picked myself back up and kept drinking, binge drinking. I was president of the Spirit Club, so I focused on it. Marching band was over and I finally graduated from Freedom High, Class of 1997.

I became assistant manager at the Morganton Recreation Department. I helped with scheduling and pool maintenance and even had keys. I opened up and closed, and also taught private swimming lessons. Life was great. We had big parties. Of course, I drank and drove, but never got caught. Then this woman named Fay accused me of stealing the canteen key. I had all door keys, so why would I steal that one? I told her to look at the person she had hired to run it. Guess what she did though? She cornered me in the canteen. Just because she was sleeping with the boss, Gary, she felt she could she run over everyone. So I threw my keys on the table and said I was DONE. I apologized to the manager, Gary, and walked out. I made an appointment with the city manager and told her what happened. She took everything off my record and swept everything else under the rug, because I knew Gary and Fay were sleeping together. I saw them in New York together. They all were scared. And I honestly didn't care because I was headed to UNC Charlotte.

An Eye Of The Storm

So fall came around and I was enrolled at UNCC. Bye Bye Miss American Pie. That was my song. He actually wrote this song while he was a patient at Broughton Hospital. This song reminds me of leaving Morganton to go off to school. Anyway, talk about a party school. I didn't go to class and partied like it was 1968. I was going to clubs, bars, and parties. One time I went to a frat party and got mono, just from sharing a cup with a stranger. I had to medically withdraw from school. Do you have any idea what that means? I had to move out of the dorms. I moved to apartments called Campus Edge in 1999, with two other guys. One of the guys, Bose, told me to quit mooching off my mom and get a job, so I did. I became a lifeguard for Charlotte Marion Diehl Center pool and also taught private swimming lessons. Things were looking up. Everywhere my friends and I went, I drove. I was always looking for love too.

I met this guy named Dennis who sexually abused me. I said no and to stop, but of course, he didn't. I was so angry that I kicked him away and drove him home. On my way back, I got pulled over! I was also a lifeguard and private swim instructor at Marion Diehl Center... I couldn't lose my job. My boss found me a good lawyer and then I, sadly, had to call my mom. By the grace of something, she saved me once again. She came to Charlotte and drove me around for a couple of weeks until I got my paper license. I only blew a .08. I was upset with Dennis and I never saw him again! Can you believe that??! I sure couldn't. I thought I did something wrong. I didn't know I was abused and didn't press charges. The officer asked, "Did something happen to me?" I said, "Yes, but don't worry about it!" Another great co-worker got me out of the holding cell in jail. I was sitting beside a real criminal. This girl's crime was she had dope in her crotch. Anyway, Mom came and booked her a hotel I ended up moving closer to my job in South Charlotte.

I got a roommate. We found an apartment. It was the year 2000. My roommate always had a party and one of her friends brought over some cocaine. I tried it and loved it. A co-worker talked to me about selling drugs since I was desperate for money. I was still trying to find love also and had a great co-worker, who was my best friend. Eric trained me so I could be stronger. Anyway, I had to go to a counselor to see if I was an alcoholic. Sure enough, I checked all of the boxes to confirm alcoholic at the age of twenty-one. Mom was coming down that weekend. When she got to my place, we went to lunch.

I told her three things... Can you guess what those three things are? I told her... I needed help, I was sexually abused, and I lost my job. For the first time, in a very long time, the weight I was carrying lifted. We did go shopping and Mom then told me to get some clothes. She brought me back home to Morganton that day. On our way home, I received a phone call; my shipment was in. I told my ex-co-worker I couldn't pick it up.

When we got home, Mom called our friend, Lory. He suggested rehab at Fellowship Hall in Greensboro, North Carolina. This is a private rehab. At the time, it was the best; still is but $64,000 now. Several stars went there; it was founded by Dorothea Dix and they didn't have an opening for two weeks. So I slept and went out to have that last hurrah before I went to rehab. I remember when I went; it was January 2001. I had to go through detox for a week. I couldn't talk to Mommy. I got through detox and went to the gym. I walked on the treadmill and you'll never guess what happened there? Try! Take a couple of guesses. I woke up on the floor with a doctor on top of me. He asked me some dumb questions, like, "Who was the president?" I didn't know. He said I had a seizure, probably from no sugar. They said it was a withdrawal seizure. I passed out all the time, so I knew better. Any, I was there twenty-eight days; best time in my life. I then came home.

I had begun a new, wonderful life. My friend Lory took me to my first AA meeting. I couldn't believe how wonderful and simple this program was. One of our FAVORITE Sayings is "Easy Does It!" I went back to school and got my degree in human services and psychology. Mom and I ended up moving to Nebo, North Carolina and moved to Lake James. For some reason, something always happened to me every time I left school early. You will never guess what? Every time I left, I was immediately behind wrecks in front of me and each time I stopped. One night, a couple of us went to see our professor play in a band and low and behold, what happened, you ask?! There was a wreck right in front of us. I stopped and ran into the first car from my car. A woman was in the driver seat. Her leg was dangling off her knee. Then I looked in the back seat. There, guess what I saw. I saw a child; she was crying and coughing. I told her mother that I couldn't move her but I needed to get the child out. The mother refused at first until I finally convinced her to let me take her daughter. I pulled the child out and made sure that she was not hurt.

The medics came and checked out the child. I knew, then, that God was calling me for great things.

It was 2007 and I was swimming all the time. I pet-sat a cat for a friend and ended up keeping her. Mokey is now nineteen years old. When we moved, I joined The Nebo Fire Department, because I am great in emergency situations, as you already know. I became a first responder. I went further with school to become a paramedic. I met a wonderful man in the department who was the forest ranger for McDowell County. I invited him to a family cookout where he met my grandma. He turned around and invited me to his church, Nebo First Baptist Church. In August 2009, we got married and I received my EMT-B license. I was nine- and-a-half years sober and felt as though I didn't need the AA program anymore. Because I suffer from Skitzo Effective Disorder and in a bad situation; Schizophrenia is different than Schizophrenia Effective disorder. Effective means that I can swing both manic and into a major depression. The bad situation is The Jim situation! He moved in with us after he got out of prison. He went to prison for molesting his stepson and also made his ex-wife crazy. It was 2013. Jim was studying to be a paramedic before he went to prison. He knew how to mentally play with someone. He played with me and made me crazy. I had to separate and get help. Can you guess what happened next?! I started drinking again. Once again, I lost control and went back to Scott, my husband, with the stipulation that I could tell this creep who was living with us to leave. Scott agreed, but my alcoholism only got worse.

Scott and I had a father/daughter relationship and I couldn't depend on him for anything. He is on the cusp of Aries and a Taurus. Plus, he has a traumatic brain injury from being in a coma as a child. I was so alone and drank to cope. Then I received a phone call from my estranged family.

Well, the phone call was from Sossman's Funeral Home where they told me that my birth mother was dead. It was kinda funny. I Knew Calvin Sossman! He knew my mommy, Gena, but never knew I was adopted. We laughed and he asked me to contact my brother and sisters that were taken away before I was born. I tried but got nowhere. I called Calvin back and he told me that Linda gave him my name. She didn't want to pay for Helen's burial, so Calvin and I decided to give verbal consent to cremate and bury her. This made me think of my father, which I finally reconnected with my father

Do you remember my father's name? Billy Black. That's right! He actually introduced me to his side of the family, which was during a New Year's celebration. I found out who I got my many talents from; also who I looked like. We are extremely talented. I have an aunt and two uncles: Carla, Aaron, and Dana, and lots of cousins. We sang and played instruments, and got full bellies. I was still angry with my father for leaving me in that hell I lived in. You see, he came to see me when I was two years old, plus he paid child support! I never saw him again. He left me behind, so, I kept my distance and kept on drinking. I was miserable.

In 2011, my body finally gave out and I couldn't lift my own head. I went to the doctor and found out I have fibromyalgia and lupus. I was so depressed, especially after I just got my EMT-B license. Once again, my life was shattered. I had to quit everything. My husband, Scott, had to take off work so he could spoon-fed me. Two weeks later, I was able to get some strength back. I called a lawyer to get put on disability, because I had no income. It took me three-and-a-half years to get a hearing. I finally received my approval. Major depression set in hard, so I drank more and more. I became a raging alcoholic, drinking every day. I had become just like my family. UGG!!! McDowell County doesn't like me much because I see them for who they are. Most have religion but not faith.

One time we were members of a local church and because Scott's ex-in-laws were big contributors, they wouldn't allow me to work with their daughter's class. That was sooo unreal, so I quit going. Scott took their side every time. I was furious. So I did the next best thing. Take a guess. Of course. I continued to drink my worries away. Scott's ex made life a living hell for me. Scott and Naomi had a daughter named Samantha. One day, Naomi decided to have a woman come over and get Samantha and take her back home to her mother. I couldn't believe it and was pissed. This cousin of Samantha's had her phone at the door and said Naomi said it was OK. I said, "No!!! We had plans!!!" The lady said, "Well, Naomi was coming to get Samantha!" I said, "Let her try!!! I'm going to call the police!!!"

Those people are crazy. Scott was at work. The police came two hours later. I didn't know what these people were capable of. Plus, they lived across the street. Gurrrr!!!!! Scott didn't want me to call police. He wanted me to bow down to them, like he did, but I refused to let that woman run all over me. Samantha decided she wasn't going to come to her dad's anymore. You see, Scott tried taking her phone away, but by then, it was too late. Samantha was fifteen. Scott thinks I'm a dumb blonde, I hate to break it to him, but, I'm a survivor.

I did cheat on him though. I was still searching for love and was lonely. I couldn't talk to Scott, and I sure as hell could not talk to Mom. Scott's always treated me less than just to make himself look good. So, once again, I drank. I had turned into a raging alcoholic, just like my family. I hated everybody and everything. I would cry constantly and was miserable. I turned to cutting myself begging for help. Scott wanted a friend of his named Jim! He molested his own stepson and even made his ex-wife crazy!!!! He was a firefighter training to be a paramedic, just like me. So he knew about medications. He convinced Scott to make a list of my meds so he could play. It worked. That's when I separated from Scott and had to be put on psych meds for about six months. Then I came back and kicked Jim out. Evil man: lied, cheated, and stole my mind.

Anyway, back to me cutting myself, as you remember. I was finally taken to the hospital in Marion and talked to a psychologist! I spoke with a psychologist and told her all I wanted was for someone to hear me. I needed rehab.

So I went to this so-called rehab in South Carolina. The person who ran it was named Jim, who was an active user and slept with the women. He owned property in Nebo, North Carolina that claimed to be a Christian-based rehab center. Scott and I have rescued several men who have lived there. Jim used them for free labor and providing them with drugs. He is still doing it today and someone needs to stop him. He is evil. I went to Green Sea, South Carolina, with Jim and his crew and saw the rehab. They get everything for free, but this man flies off the handle in rages. He provides them with money and with drugs. And, he buddied up to the women to have sex with. He is endangering the welfare of others. Go figure. Another Jim. I had Scott to come and get me at the end of the week.

That's when we started rescuing. I drank and partied with them. This Shawn guy was the best manipulator of women. He made women feel sorry for him; I emotionally cheated with them all. Then, there was Ron. I got him housing. He was hottt. Again, I emotionally cheated on Scott with him He and I would drink together and talk. He would listen, just like the rest of Jim's crew. I just found out that Ron got married and has property in Marion. So, I begged to go to rehab again. This time, I went to Turning Point, all the way to Georgia. I was in the middle of a hurricane. That was so much FUN. I had to leave on day 22 because Medicare wouldn't pay anymore, so I completed the program. The year was 2017. I was sober for about three months, but I, still, didn't go to meetings. Just dried OUT. I soon picked the bottle back up again I was ANGRY AND PISSED OFF AT THE WORLD. I was arguing with Scott. He drank with me but Scott's answer to everything was church.

Scott is one of those who has religion rather than faith. We went to a church in Marion Called Garden Creek Baptist Church in 2018. The pastor there was the biggest con of them all. His name was Pastor Don. He and his wife are on SUBOXONE. Suboxone is an opioid that is supposed to help one get off another addiction such as heroin. They had to feed their addiction. I knew he had a relationship with my best friend and she is married too. I did try Suboxone for a while because I was in so much physical pain. If you remember, I have fibromyalgia and lupus.

Back to Don; he asked to borrow $1800. He still owes us seventeen hundred. One of the deacons, there, is footing his bills, to this day. And that deacon and his wife are also doped up, from pain medication. So they love Don. The town of Marion keeps quiet and doesn't say anything! I have told the others, but they can't do anything. Because Ray is the head deacon. What do you think I did next? I picked myself up, then I left the church. What do you think Scott did?! He stayed. I told Scott I would go to church with him if he left Garden Creek. I drank more and more and He did not leave for another six months. Scott wanted me to stay home so he drank with me. I begged again; I needed REHAB. Mommy came to my rescue.....again. She found a place in Pilot Mountain, North Carolina. This treatment center is called Hope Valley. Scott and I took a trip to Gatlinburg, Tennessee. One Last DRUNK!!!!!! I planned to stop and had my date set. That weekend was great. We went to a psychic!!! I was looking for anyone to help Scott and me! I thought Scott may listen to her! She was great, true and faith-based. So far everything she said was going to happen has. I, OF COURSE, then.... then, the year 2020 came around.

I never STOPPED DRINKING. I begged again to go to go to rehab, as you already know. Mommy and I sat on the phone with each other. She found Hope Valley. They wanted me to go to detox first, but I said no. Normally someone would go in withdrawals so bad that they need medical help! Detox was a waste of my time! So....? Guess what they did. They had me to stay sober for one week. They told me to call everyday so that I held my responsibility. Of course, I didn't stay sober. No one, except for Scott knew this. I guess when this book is published, they will know. But, I knew that I didn't need detox. Plus, I couldn't AFFORD IT. So then I went to Hope Valley and left for rehab on January 7th. When we got there, I met with my counselor and she was hard core. Mom and her already clashed. The other counselor told me to have Mommy call everyday as well. They butted heads. Holy cow. Mommy called me before and told me that my counselor was something else. I actually really like her. Anyway, we finally got there after missing a turn or two. The house was beautiful, an old farm house. Scott helped bring my luggage in. You see, I came in with broken ribs because I fell off a porch but I never went to the hospital. I couldn't afford it! So, I couldn't lift anything. I sat with my counselor and she went over all the rules. I asked about one. We were not to speak with any of the men! Nor were we to make eye contact! I felt that was being disrespectful. She said, "You're married. You have no business talking to men!" Needless to say, I put my head down every time that I passed by a man. I did not want to get kicked out.

I had to set an alarm and had to make sure I was up by 6:30 am. I made my bed and even had to get dressed!!! I had class all morning and then counseling!!! We only had five of us that were there, which means we had lots of personal, one-to-one time with the counselors. I was just in for two weeks when something happened. Can you guess what it was??! Give it a shot. I fell off a step. I really hurt my foot! I hobbled up, crawling back up to the house. I was going to class. It was 11:00 a.m. The counselor is a retired nurse, so she took me to the hospital in Mt. Airy. We had to sit in the waiting room for six and a half hours. Finally I was taken back, but still had to wait in the ER lobby. Finally, a nurse practitioner took a look at me; my counselor and I were beside a man who was bleeding from his cheek. Someone stitched him up in front of us. Talk about HIPPA violation. They finally got back to me and took me for X-rays. Try guessing what I had???

I broke my left ankle. The day was January twenty-third and the doctor put a cast on and gave me crutches. My counselor had to ask someone to show me how to use them. I weighed 184 pounds. The one who showed me didn't even put the correct height on the crutches, so we made it back to the house. Because I could no longer climb steps, I had to be discharged that night So, they called my mommy and husband. Scott had to come get me that night The house parent had to pack up my belongings and helped Scott load up the car. They even helped me get in. Scott drove us home and we went to BED. The next day we went to emerge ortho. They unwrapped my ankle and it was HUGE. They took X-rays and said it was a clean break. They then fit me into a boot and I was miserable. My ankle slowly got better after our new pastor prayed over me. I got up from my wheelchair and started walking on it. My ankle healed quicker than expected. By March, I was out of the boot. If you truly have faith in God, He created a miracle that day.

I started going to AA again. My favorite old-timers were there. I was afraid all of them were dead. I asked so many times for a sponsor; finally I found a great one! AA is such a blessing. Thank you, Bill W. and Dr. Silk Worth. They are who founded Alcoholics Anonymous.

Today, I'm over five months clean and sober. My sobriety birthday is January 23rd, 2020. I am truly A GRATEFUL RECOVERING ALCOHOLIC. I picked up my ninety-day chip It's red. The saying is "Now!? We Have Blood Back In Our Alcohol Stream" My faith has grown considerably. I'm now a proud member of State Street Church Of God. Can you guess where my pastor is from??! BISHOP WADE is from Germany. Funny. I knew I liked him for a reason. HaHaHa!!! I'm about to be publishing my book. I did do ONE BAD THING.

I fell at my neighbor's house. I was trying to ask if their daughter would like a job feeding out animals so we can take off for the weekend. The neighbors do not like me because I'm sober And THEY ARE NOT. I re-injured my ankle, tore the ligaments, three of them. I went to the hospital in Marion; that was on May 7th, a week after my birthday. I was so upset. I have started booking for teaching swimming lessons when this happened.

Today is May 28th. I'm starting to be able to walk on my foot again. I'm getting a job soon. I'm working out with my personal trainer because I'm not in great shape. I continue to lose weight and am only 115 pounds now. My body is so frail and I had to get a new doctor. I went to my old one, Dr. Davis, and she refused to see me. I think I was in the middle of an office spat because I saw one nurse practitioner that was wonderful. Then I saw another nurse practitioner named Crystal and she was livid. She would not hear anything I had to say. I asked for a full blood work and she wouldn't do it.

Then, I asked to talk to Dr. Davis I'm guessing that she is retiring and she would not see me. So, I reported the issue and had my files transferred to my new doctor.

My husband Scott, you ask?? He is finally getting help and seeing a counselor. I am not going to continue having a father/daughter relationship. He has to get a sponsor in AA. He has to go to counseling or... I am going to leave him. I am forty-two years old now. My sobriety is coming first, no matter what I have to do. I am a survivor.

Today I am building a relationship with my father. I call him Daddy now!!! I understand his role. He did not want to mess with my estranged family. DSS intervened during my adoption and told him not to try to stop it

For my forty-second birthday, we celebrated at my mom's. Since Mother's Day falls along my birthday, we celebrate my birthday and Mother's Day together. I am, also, GETTING READY to start recording music. I'm harmonizing well with the leader of Shattered Glass. I am in the process of getting a part-time job!!? I have to get enough money for a pool, as my body can't physically, mentally, or emotionally heal without chlorine.

As you remember, I have fibromyalgia and lupus! I also have been diagnosed with osteoporosis! Even though my body is falling apart, I am so thankful. One piece of advice I wanna share is "NEVER UNDERESTIMATE THE POWER OF GOD!!!!!!!" The Lord Is great, BEYOND Everything ELSE. MAY GOD BLESS EACH AND EVERY ONE OF YOU.

God, Grant me the Serenity, to accept the things I cannot change... Courage to change the Things I Can... and the Wisdom to know the Difference!!!

www.ingramcontent.com/pod-product-compliance
Ingram Content Group UK Ltd.
Pitfield, Milton Keynes, MK11 3LW, UK
UKHW022208230426
12048UKWH00016BA/726